EXTREME SPORTS BIOGRAPHIES™

TAÏG KHRIS
IN-LINE SKATING SUPERSTAR

AARON ROSENBERG

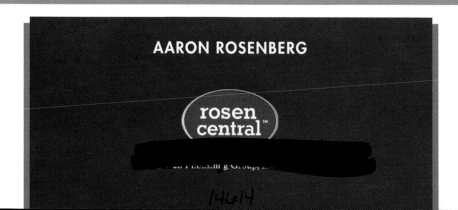

rosen
central™

Published in 2005 by The Rosen Publishing Group, Inc.
29 East 21st Street, New York, NY 10010

Library of Congress Cataloging-in-Publication Data

Rosenberg, Aaron.
Taïg Khris / by Aaron Rosenberg.
    p. cm. — (Extreme sports biographies)
Summary: A biography of the Algerian-born in-line skating champion, focusing on the tricks and stunts he performed at the X-Games and other competitions.
Includes bibliographical references.
ISBN 1-4042-0069-X (lib. bdg.)
1. Khris, Taïg, 1975--—Juvenile literature. 2. Roller skaters—Algeria—Biography—Juvenile literature. 3. In-line skating—Juvenile literature.
[1. Khris, Taïg, 1975– 2. Roller skaters. 3. In-line skating. 4. Extreme sports.]
I. Title. II. Series: Extreme sports biographies (Rosen Publishing Group)
GV858.22.K47R67 2004
796.21'092–dc22

                                            2003022030

Manufactured in the United States of America

On the cover: Left: Taïg Khris during competition at the 2001 X Games. Right: Taïg Khris photographed in 2003 in Paris, France.

CONTENTS

In-line skating was invented as a way for ice skaters to practice skating in the off-season and off the ice. To many, that's all in-line skates will ever be—a tool to help practice for another sport. But over the last twenty years, in-line skating has become a sport of its own. People have demonstrated that the sport has its own tricks, tips, and stunts. Taïg Khris has helped prove that.

Khris has only been a professional skater since 1997, but he is considered one of the greatest athletes in the sport. It's not just the fact that he's won so many medals, either, although Khris has won every major title in the sport and has earned a medal in almost every event he's entered. Taïg Khris is more than that. In addition to being an athlete, he is a talented magician, a pianist, a champion tennis player, and a skilled dancer. He has even taken up acting!

This is one of the reasons why Khris is such a fan favorite. He has many talents, and he brings all of them together with his skating—his grace, his skill, his flair for the dramatic, and his drive to succeed. Khris demonstrates that people can really do almost anything they set their mind to, and he never stops trying to do better in every aspect of his life.

Taïg Khris has more tricks up his sleeve than just a few great moves. In addition to owning skate-related businesses in Paris and West Palm Beach, Florida, Khris is branching out into an acting career.

CHAPTER ONE
BEGINNINGS

Taïg Khris was born in Algeria on July 27, 1975. His father is Greek and his mother is French. Taïg grew up speaking both languages and learning both cultures. He attended school but did not excel, and he seemed to have no real direction to his life. His parents often wondered what he would wind up doing for a career.

Khris had no doubts, however. He'd known what he wanted to do from the moment he tried on his first pair of skates. Taïg was six when he first started skating. He and his family were living in Paris by then. Taïg and his

In-line skaters use the half-pipe for jumps and airborne tricks.

• •

brother used to roller-skate everywhere. They would spend the entire day racing around on their skates. Eventually they started trying to do jumps as well. As he grew older, Taïg built his own ramps and jumps, and taught himself how to handle them. He became good at roller-skating and at a variety of jumps and tricks. All of his skating was in the streets, though, and on found obstacles or the ones he built himself.

Taïg was fifteen before he encountered his first pro-fessionally made skate ramp in 1990. It was a half-pipe,

The First In-line Athletes

Taïg Khris entered the sport of in-line skating in 1997. Many skaters had gotten there before him, though. These skaters helped pave the way for Taïg and those after him. A few of the first in-line skaters are the following:

Tom Fry: Born and raised in Australia, Fry won the gold medal in the vert at the first X Games in 1995. He is considered one of the first in-line pros, and he invented many of the tricks still used today.

Cesar Mora: Born on February 5, 1975, in Madrid, Spain, Mora grew up in Sydney, Australia. Only 5 feet, 5 inches (1.65 meters) in height, Mora started skating in 1993 and began competing a year later. He won the silver medal in the vert competition at the first X Games in 1995.

Manuel Billiris: Born in Darwin, Australia, on September 25, 1975, Billiris has been competing in in-line skating since 1994. He won the bronze in vert at the first X Games; he won the silver in the high-air competition that same year.

Chris Edwards: Born on December 22, 1973, in Minneapolis, Minnesota, Edwards took third place in vert at the X Games in both 1996 and 1997. In 1997, he got beaten out of second place by newcomer Taïg Khris.

Fabiola da Silva: Born in São Paulo, Brazil, on June 12, 1979, Fabiola is only 5 feet, 2 inches (1.6 m) tall, and weighs a little more than 100 pounds (45 kilograms). Da Silva is one of the few female pro skaters in the world. She took the gold in the women's vert at the X Games six times in the last eight years.

and he immediately fell in love with it. He taught himself to handle the half-pipe, then the vert (vertical) ramp and other forms. A whole new world had opened up for him.

A few months later, Khris attended a competition in Germany. It was the first time he had met other serious skaters, many of whom were already skating celebrities—Raphael Sandoz, René Hulgreen, Marcos Longares, and Toto, to name a few. Taïg's parents and brother hadn't understood his fascination with skating. His friends and classmates had not understood his dedication. But these other skaters understood. For the first time, Taïg found himself part of a group. They shared one thing—a love of skating. No one was sponsoring skaters at the time, so it wasn't money that drew any of them. It was just sheer enjoyment.

In 1996, Taïg's world got even better. In-line skates were already available around the world. But now roller skaters were discovering them. People started switching to in-lines, and Taïg and his friends quickly found out why. They could move faster on in-line skates and could perform more tricks with them, especially off the ramp. The world of in-line skating had begun. Taïg Khris had finally found his career.

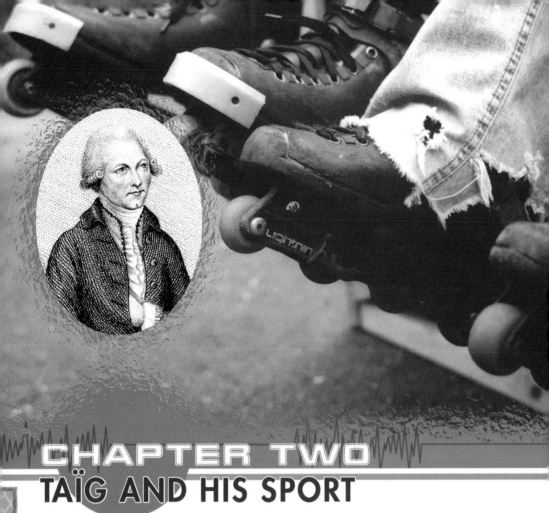

CHAPTER TWO
TAÏG AND HIS SPORT

Taïg entered in-line skating at the perfect time. The sport itself was just beginning to take off. Taïg was in the best position to help develop it and to make it more visible and more popular. In-line skating didn't spring out of nowhere, of course. It grew out of more traditional roller-skating, the same activity Taïg and his brother used to practice every day.

Roller skates themselves date back to the 1760s. That was when a man named John Joseph Merlin, a Belgian inventor and designer of musical instruments,

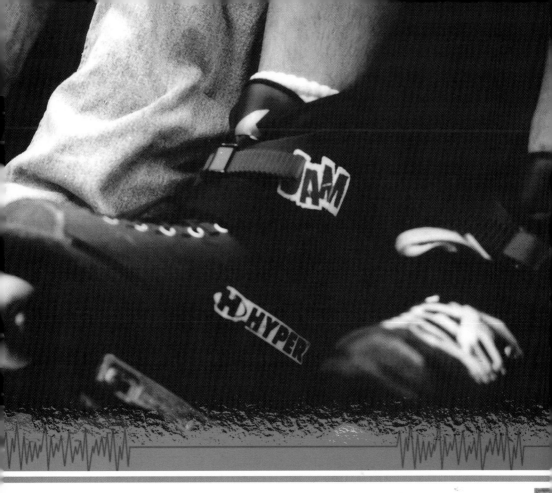

Belgian inventor John Joseph Merlin, left inset, invented the roller skate in 1760. Pictured above is its modern cousin, the in-line skate.

• •

had an interesting idea. He took a pair of ice skates and attached small metal wheels to them so he could skate on land. Unfortunately for Merlin, he had not considered the need for brakes and wound up skating into a large mirror, shattering it, and wounding himself in the process. But the idea about skating remained, and over time it was refined and improved. By 1840, roller skates were popular in Germany, and in the 1900s they arrived in the United States, causing roller rinks to open all across the country. These skates had a front brake and four wheels, and the

design didn't change much for the next eight decades. In 1960, the Chicago Skate Company produced an in-line skate, but the skate was too uncomfortable, too unstable, and too difficult to brake. It didn't catch on.

Then, in 1979, a young Minneapolis hockey player named Scott Olson found one of the Chicago in-line skates in a used sporting goods store. He realized that these skates might allow him to train for hockey during the summer, when ice was scarce. So he bought them. Olson's new skates didn't work as well as he wanted, so he modified them. He reset the wheels and added a heel brake. A few years later, in 1984, a Minneapolis businessman named Bob Naegele Jr. purchased the company Olson had started. Naegele began selling the in-line skates by the boxful. That company became Rollerblade Inc., which has remained one of the leading in-line skate manufacturers. Rollerblade sponsored a young unknown named Taïg Khris in 1997.

In-line is one of the newest sports—it has only existed since the late 1990s. In some ways, that's a good thing. All of the professional athletes are still young and energetic, and they feel they have something to prove. But being the new kid on the block isn't always easy. A lot of people think in-line skating is a joke, something too easy

Before in-line skates were in wide use, roller skates were popular. New York City in 1979 was the epicenter of the roller disco craze.

Skate Type

In-line skating is a popular sport, in part because it is so versatile. Different people skate in different ways and for different purposes. Each type of skating requires a slightly different skate.

Aggressive skating: This is skating for competition. Aggressive skates are for tricks and stunts. Vert skating is a type of aggressive skating, as is park skating. Aggressive skates are tough, durable skates. They are usually made of thick, hard plastic. They have small wheels for maneuverability. The skate boot sole is a metal grind plate that protects the boots during stunts. The major manufacturers of aggressive skates are Able Frames, Dahan, Deshi, Fiziks Frames, GC Frames, Kizer Frames, K2, Remz, Roces, Rollerblade, Salomon, and USD.

Artistic figure skating: Figure roller-skating, roller-dancing, and synchronized roller-skating can be done on either quad roller skates or artistic in-line skates. Quads are actually more common for this type of skating, though some people will use in-lines instead. These skates tend to be lighter in weight and built for maneuverability. They don't have the protection of the aggressive skates.

Recreational skates: Not everyone skates for competition. Some people just skate for fun. These skates tend to be reasonably light. They also have larger and softer wheels than the more competitive models, because comfort is more important than speed or accuracy.

Hockey skates: Ice hockey players still use in-line skates for practice in the off-season, but people also play hockey with

Women compete at the Speed Skating World Championships in Barquisimeto, Venezuela, in November 2003.

in-line skates today. These skates are solidly built and generally have a flat-profiled wheel for added stability.

Speed skates: True speed skates are very lightweight, have little or no ankle support, minimal or no boot padding, a long wheelbase, and either four or five wheels. A lot of companies manufacture speed skates, including both Salomon and Rollerblade.

Quad roller skates: Quad roller skates are the traditional roller skates that everyone used before the in-line skates were perfected. They have four (or sometimes six) wheels set in pairs down the foot, and either a front brake, a heel brake, or both. Quad skates are still used for artistic competitions and for roller-dancing. Some people do quad aggressive skating, however. Taïg Khris first learned to skate on quads and only later switched to in-lines. Most aggressive quad skaters build their own skates by buying regular skates and then reinforcing them. The major quad roller skate manufacturers are Formula, Pacer, Riedell, and Roller Derby.

and too immature to count as a sport of its own. Skateboarders mock in-liners and often give them a hard time at skate parks. One of the reasons for this is that in-line skating has become popular with nonskaters. Especially in Europe, entire families often go skating together. After all, in-line skates can be used by anyone from the very young to the very old—it isn't as physically taxing as riding a bike, and it isn't as difficult as skateboarding for maintaining stability and speed. Thousands of people skate around Paris every Friday. This is a wonderful boost for the sport in general. Other "extreme sports" may see in-lines as less edgy, because children, parents, and even grandparents are out there using them instead of just serious athletes.

That kind of bad attitude has been changing, however, in large part thanks to people like Taïg Khris. At competitions like the X Games and the Gravity Games, Khris and his peers have demonstrated that in-line is not to be taken lightly. Their daring and technical expertise have won many fans, and a lot of people have admitted that the sport is every bit as exciting and challenging as skateboarding, BMX, or any of the other extreme sports.

These skaters continue to push the envelope. Taïg has said that he will build bigger and better ramps. He wants to use them for more complicated tricks. He's determined to win people's respect. Not for himself, though—with all his medals and titles, he has earned everyone's admiration. Instead, he wants people to respect the sport. He plans to show them over and over

In-line skating isn't just fun and games. French police on in-line skates patrol the streets of Paris in June 1998. Trained by a top French speed skater, the eight-man squad is picked on the basis of skating ability.

again that in-line really is interesting and challenging and innovative. He wants them to really believe him.

SAFETY FIRST

Aggressive in-line skating is an extreme sport. One of the factors of an extreme sport is the amount of risk its athletes take. Vert skating, in particular, carries a high risk of

injury. The skaters race up a ramp that rises to a vertical pitch—straight up! Once launched into the air, the skaters perform tricks 8 feet (2.4 m) or more above the ground. A fall from that height can easily break bones or rupture organs. This danger makes it very important for skaters to take proper safety measures. It's OK for the sport to be exciting and daring, but if you get hurt you can't skate at all. That isn't any fun.

Helmets

Skaters use the same helmets as bikers and skateboarders. Helmets come in a variety of colors and patterns, but the shape is always roughly the same. A good helmet is properly certified by either the American National Standards Institute (ANSI), the Snell Memorial Foundation, the Canadian Standards Association (CSA), or the American Society for Testing and Materials (ASTM). If the helmet does not have approval from at least one of these organizations on its packaging, don't buy it. The helmet should fit comfortably—snug enough that it won't slip or slide but loose enough that it doesn't hurt. It should not restrict your vision at all. Taïg Khris takes safety seriously. That's why he hasn't been seriously injured. The following list includes the types of safety gear Khris and other skaters wear for protection.

Taïg Khris competes at the Hermosa Beach Bash in Hermosa Beach, California, in June 2001. Before he gets airborne, Taïg Khris takes proper safety precautions.

Knee Pads

These should be made of strong but flexible plastic. Knee pads need to fit snugly. The straps should be tight enough to hold them in place but loose enough that they don't cut off blood circulation.

Elbow Pads

These are similar to knee pads, and you should look for the same things when buying them—sturdy but flexible, snug but not too tight.

Gloves

Unlike biking, skating does not require you to hold anything with your hands. You don't even need to worry about gripping your board the way skateboarders do. So you can concentrate on getting gloves that will protect your hands if you fall, rather than ones that give you a lot of flexibility and control. Go for good thick gloves with plenty of padding. Leather works well.

Skate Liners

Skate liners come in several types, but the best are the ones that lace up. These provide more support and a better fit, because you can adjust them each time you wear them. These may not seem like safety gear, but they are. A good

A helmet, gloves, elbow pads, and knee pads are essential for in-line skaters. This is especially true for high-risk vert skating.

Taïg Khris works the half-pipe at the National In-line Skating Series contest in Los Angeles, California, in June 1999.

skate liner keeps the skate on your foot more securely, allowing you more control. That means you're less likely to fall, because the skate does what you want it to do.

Taïg's Stunt-Practicing Motto

Like all pro skaters, Taïg practices stunts before he tries them on a ramp. He works out the stunt on the ground first. Taïg does this step by step. He makes sure he knows exactly what he's trying to do and how to do it. For yourself, get the steps down and the body movements. Once you're sure you understand the trick fully, you can try it for real.

If you have a foam pit near you, that makes things even easier. The soft foam pit allows you to practice a ramp trick, and if you fall, you'll avoid hurting yourself. Foam pits are still rare, and a lot of skate parks don't have them yet. If that's the case at your skate park, just work on getting as much of the stunt down before you ever leave the ground.

CHAPTER THREE
PROFESSIONAL LIFE

In 1997, Khris took part in his first in-line skating competition. Most professional athletes spend years competing and hoping to catch the interest of a sponsor. Not Khris. After the finals, the Rollerblade company representative approached Khris and offered him a contract. He was now a professional.

Of course, that meant a lot of life changes. The first was that Khris suddenly found himself traveling a lot. He had made a few trips before, but Rollerblade was sending him to competitions all over Europe. This meant he spent a

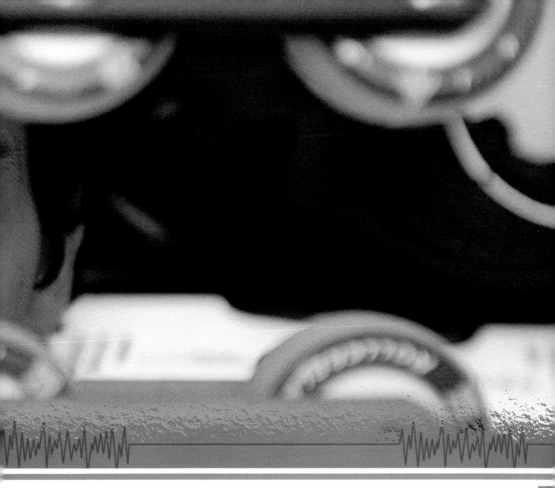

Taïg Khris seen through the blades that made him famous. As a professional skater, he has the opportunity to travel around the world.

lot of time away from his family. But the biggest change was language. Khris had been born in Algeria and raised in Paris. He was a native French speaker and didn't know a word of English. So, in addition to the usual training on skates, Khris also found himself studying a new language. It was difficult, but Khris managed it, quickly becoming able to speak comfortably with English and American journalists. He also settled into the role of a skating professional.

One of the most exciting things for Khris was having the time to practice new tricks. He and his peers were the

first in-line athletes, which meant they were creating a lot of their tricks from scratch. Before this, most of their tricks had been adapted from skateboarding, but the two sports were not identical and the difference in equipment made it hard to translate. Now Khris and the others had the chance to work on new tricks specifically designed for in-line skates, and people began to sit up and take notice. The sport was quickly gaining recognition and popularity. Khris was right at the forefront.

Over the next six years, he became one of the most famous and most successful in-line skaters. He added Club Med, Yoo-Hoo, and Haribo to his list of sponsors. Everyone wanted a piece of him and for good reason. Khris won every major title in the sport, in competitions including the X Games, the world championships, the Aggressive Skaters Association (ASA) Tour Championships, and the Gravity Games. Out of his first 103 competitions, he placed first a staggering 71 times, second 15 times, and third 14 times. He won medals in all but three of those events!

Khris's success stemmed in part from his determination and his willingness to spend long hours on each trick to make sure he got it right. His years skating in Paris on quad skates made him extremely comfortable on skates. That translated to in-line skates when he

---

Before Taïg Khris performs his signature moves in competition, he reworks them again and again. Captured at work in July 2003, Khris practices on a half-pipe in Paris.

Sponsors

Taïg Khris has four sponsors: Rollerblade, Yoo-Hoo, Haribo, and Club Med. Rollerblade was responsible for making him a professional in-line skater—it offered him a place on its team after his first competition back in 1997. The other three came later. Taïg is most active with Club Med and teaches a skate camp for the company every year. He often goes to Club Med in Florida to practice during the winter, because it has a complete indoor skate park, where he can practice all year. As part of Yoo-Hoo's team, he participates in the Aggressive Skaters Association's Pro Tour and in other tours that Yoo-Hoo organizes, such as the ASA High School series, which goes to various high schools across the country.

Khris skated to a first place finish in the Aggressive In-line Vertical Finals during the August 2001 X Games in Philadelphia, Pennsylvania.

switched over. Watching Khris skate, it seems as if he were born to the skates, as if he preferred skating to walking—and perhaps he does. But Khris's success also grew out of his sheer talent. He had a grace and speed few other skaters could match and the precision to make difficult tricks seem almost effortless. Most athletes have good days and bad days and even an inconsistent season or two. Khris is the exception. He has proven to be one of the most consistent athletes in the sport, perhaps in most sports. Every time he takes part in an event, he impresses both the fans and the judges with his skill, his daring, and his control.

The Magician

Most athletes have nicknames, and some of them for the strangest reasons. It might be something they said once, something about their appearance, or something about the way they handle themselves when competing.

Taïg Khris is often referred to as the Magician. Most people think that's because he seems almost magical on his skates. Watching him on the ramps, it looks like he can defy gravity and stop time. Certainly his skill makes the almost impossible look practically easy, and that is one definition of magic. But that isn't where Khris gets his nickname.

Actually, his nickname has a very simple explanation. Khris really is a magician. Not the kind who turns people into frogs, but the kind who pulls rabbits out of hats. As a youth, Khris became fascinated with street

Khris takes a moment out of his busy schedule to relax in his home city, Paris.

---

magicians, the people who perform magic tricks on the sidewalk for money. Street magic doesn't require complicated props or expensive equipment—it's all about style, speed, and sleight of hand. Making a full-size airplane disappear requires a lot of time and money and setup. But making a coin vanish or restoring a shredded playing card just needs dexterity, showmanship, and talent. Khris decided to learn this art and showed his usual intense focus. In no time, he was impressing family and friends with his tricks. As he grew older, rather than setting the hobby aside, Khris became even more adept, mastering the skills of the street magician.

CHAPTER FOUR
IN-LINE AT THE X GAMES

For the past eight years, extreme sports' biggest and best competition has been the X Games. Aggressive in-line skating has been a part of this competition from the very beginning. This goes back to the year 1995 when Tom Fry took the gold on the vert and Cesar Mora won the silver. Two years later, a newcomer named Taïg Khris showed up and claimed second place in the event. It took him four more years, but in 2001 he finally took the gold. Even though it took him some time to win the top medal, the

A view of BMX dirt jumping and vert ramp practice at the August 2003 X Games, held at the Staples Center in Los Angeles, California

fact that Khris was able to win second place at the most prestigious event in the sport, in his first year as a professional athlete, made everyone sit up and take notice. That's why the Aggressive Skaters Association (ASA) named him Rookie of the Year in 1997. Khris's skill, enthusiasm, and potential were staggering. The sport itself was still new enough that it didn't have established athletes. Khris's impressive beginning quickly made him one of the most successful in-line skaters, as well as a fan favorite.

X Games History

The first Extreme Games were held in Newport, Rhode Island, and at Mount Snow, Vermont, from June 24 to July 1, 1995. They were organized by ESPN as a way to showcase alternative, or extreme, sports. Nine different sports were represented. Almost 200,000 people attended. That was enough to convince ESPN to repeat the event the following year. ESPN shortened the name, however, and called the event the X Games. The first half was held in Rhode Island again. But for the second year, ESPN added a winter version. The first Winter X Games were held at the Snow Summit Mountain Resort in Big Bear Lake, California, from January 30 through February 2, 1997. The summer half became known as the Summer X Games.

In 1997, the Summer X Games were moved to San Diego, California. The following year, the Winter X Games moved to Crested Butte, Colorado. Then, in 1999, the summer games moved to San Francisco. The events continue to move around—in 2001 and 2002, the summer games were in Philadelphia, while the winter games moved to Aspen, Colorado, in 2003. Each set of games stays in its new location for only two years to keep things interesting.

The Summer X Games are traditionally more popular than the winter games, drawing more than 200,000 people each year. The Winter X Games usually draw around 30,000 people, although the numbers have reached as high as 83,000 (in 2000, when it was held at Mount Snow, Vermont, again).

X Games Year-Round

The Summer X Games include the following sports: Bicycle Stunt (Vert, Dirt, Street/Stunt Park, Flatland, Downhill), Big-Air Snowboarding, Motocross (Freestyle, Step Up, Big Air), Bungee Jumping, Skysurfing, Street Luge (Dual, Mass, Super Mass, King of the Hill), Skateboard (Vert Singles, Vert Doubles, Street/Park, Vert Best Trick, Street Best Trick), Sportclimbing (Difficulty, Speed), the X-Venture Race, In-line Skating (Combined Vert, Street/Park, Vert Triples, Downhill), and Watersports (Barefoot Waterski Jumping, Wakeboarding).

The Winter X Games have the following: CrossOver, Skiboarding, Ice Climbing (Difficulty, Speed), Skiing (Big Air, Skier X, SuperPipe, Slopestyle), Snowboarding (Big Air, Boarder X, Half-pipe, Super-pipe, Slopestyle), Super-modified Shovel Racing, Snow Mountain Bike Racing (Downhill, Speed, Biker X), Snomobiling (Snocross, Hillcross), Ultracross, and Motocross (Big Air).

Blair Morgan leads the pack in the Snomobile Snocross in the 2003 X Games held in Aspen, Colorado.

More recently, ESPN has added the X Trials, where athletes compete to qualify for the X Games. There is also the X Games Road Show, a two-day interactive show that travels around the country. The Xperience is the newest showcasing of extreme sports talent, a promotional tour for the X Games.

Admittedly, Khris has not won a medal at the X Games since 2001. But that is not because he has become any less of a skater. He injured himself during the Gravity Games in 2002. The injury forced him to withdraw from the X Games that year, even though he had been the favored contender. By 2003, Khris had returned to active competition, but his injury may have slowed him down slightly. Another factor, however, is that two new skaters, Takeshi and Eito Yasutoko, had entered the sport since Khris's debut and were performing exciting new tricks. One of the reasons athletes like the Yasutokos were drawn to the sport was that they had watched skaters in the previous X Games and were excited about the sport and its possibilities. One of the people they watched was Khris himself, which means that he is partially responsible for creating his own competition. But Khris does not see that as a bad thing. Having other skilled athletes to compete against just forces him to work that much harder and to do the best he can possibly do. That's what the X Games, and the sport in general, are all about.

Best of the Best

Taïg Khris is considered one of the best in-line vert skaters in the world. But he's not alone at the top. Several other

Marc Englehart captured in motion during the 2002 X Games in Philadelphia, Pennsylvania

athletes have demonstrated amazing talent, skill, daring, and persistence in the sport. These are the people Khris measures himself against. Together they are the athletes pushing the sport of in-line skating to its limit.

Marc Englehart: Born in Sellersville, Pennsylvania, on February 2, 1983, Englehart was the first American to win a medal in the vert at the X Games since Chris

Eito Yasutoko takes a spill on the ground during the finals of the September 2003 Gravity Games' Aggressive In-line Vert competition.

Edwards in 1997. He won the gold in vert at the 2002 Gravity Games. This win made him the first American to win a major vert competition since Chris Edwards in 1994.

Eito Yasutoko: Yasutoko was born in Osaka, Japan, on July 29, 1983. Eito, nicknamed Eight, has been skating since 1992 and competing since 1995. Eito took the gold in vert at the X Games in both 1999 and 2000. He took the silver in both 2002 and 2003. Eito also won golds in every Mobile Skatepark Series (MSS) vert event in 2003. Eito and Taïg Khris have been the two athletes who have consistently added new twists to the classic flat spin.

Takeshi Yasutoko: Born in Osaka on June 25, 1986, Takeshi has actually been skating and competing as long as his older brother Eito—he was nine when he entered his first competition! Nicknamed Samurai, Takeshi took the gold in vert at the X Games in 2002, beating out his older brother (Khris had bowed out that year, due to an earlier injury). He also took the gold in vert at the 2003 Global X Games.

Shane Yost: Born in Tasmania on July 6, 1977, Yost is considered one of the most consistent athletes in skating. He is famous for his spins, and he usually places in the top three. His nickname is the Tasmanian Devil.

CHAPTER FIVE
MASTER OF THE FLAT SPIN

In an individual sport like in-line skating, athletes make their marks in three ways: precision, flair, and innovation. Precision is how well they can perform their tricks, how much control they demonstrate over themselves and their equipment, and how crisply they can execute each move. Flair is their style and grace, how smoothly they perform, and how much personality they bring to their performance. An athlete can be extremely precise but have no flair, in which case his or her tricks are technically perfect but lifeless. Another could be weak on precision but have

With a double backflip, Khris earned first place in the Aggressive In-line Vertical Finals during the 2001 X Games.

tremendous flair, meaning that the person's tricks are not perfectly executed but he or she is engaging and personable and has a distinct style. Taïg Khris is extremely precise and has a great deal of flair—the best of both worlds.

The third element to a great athlete is innovation. This is how creative the athlete is and how far he or she pushes the limit of the sport. For a sport like in-line skating, that centers around the tricks. Skaters are constantly trying to come up with new tricks or to add new twists to existing ones. Inventing a trick means that you get to name it. This

lets the skater put a permanent mark on the sport. Demonstrating a new trick and performing it well in competition show that the skater is creative, original, and striving for more. This impresses judges. It often becomes a competition of who has come up with the best new trick and performed it most smoothly. One of the keys to Khris's success is his ability to create astounding new tricks. Most athletes have a specialty—one focuses on air tricks while another works with ollie variations. Khris's specialty is the flat spin, and he has invented several variations, each one earning him more fame and new awards.

In skating language, vertical rotation is called a "flip" and horizontal rotation is a "spin." A flat spin is basically a horizontal backflip. The number in front of the name indicates the number of times the skater spins. For example, a 540 is a half spin. Eito Yasutoko's 1080 flat spin, currently the most complex flat spin ever performed, combines a half horizontal spin and a half vertical spin (540 + 540 = 1080). The skater usually starts in the forward position, spins, and lands backward.

One of the things that impresses everyone about Khris is how easy he makes each trick appear. This includes how he can perform the tricks over and over without fail. At the 2001 Summer X Games in Philadelphia, for

Taïg Khris defends his title in the In-line Vert preliminaries at the 2002 Gravity Games in Cleveland, Ohio.

History of the Flat Spin

The flat spin first appeared at the National In-line Skate Series (NISS) Championship in 1996. Unfortunately, a Danish skater named René Hulgreen performed at that same competition, and his flip tricks made everyone forget about the flat spin. The following year, Taïg Khris created the 540 flat spin and used that trick to win every competition he entered. Others soon tried this maneuver, and by the end of the year, the 540 flat spin was the new sensation in in-line skating.

In January 1998, Eito Yasutoko of Japan performed his own variation of the 540 flat spin, adding an additional reverse flip. His daring won him the International In-line Skate Series in Brazil, beating Taïg Khris by a narrow margin. Later that year, Jonathan Bergeron of Canada created the 720 flat spin and won the Best Trick category at the ASA World Championship in Las Vegas. Taïg Khris then created the 900 flat spin (adding an additional spin to the trick). He did not get the chance to perform it at the 1999 X Games, however, and Eito Yasutoko won for his version of the 720.

In November 1999, at the Asian X Games, Shane Yost performed both an improved 900 and a reverse 720. He won the show easily. A few months later, in January 2000, the skaters gathered for the Next Generation World Hobby Fair in Osaka, Japan. Eito surprised everyone with his newest trick: the 1080 flat spin. He performed it beautifully, stunning spectators and judges alike, and easily won the competition.

The flat spin continues to evolve, as each skater tries to top those who came before. In 2002, at the Gravity Games, Taïg Khris added yet another wrinkle, by performing the first-ever double flat spin. How will this trick grow next?

example, Khris performed a perfect backflip in the first round. That trick was impressive enough, but in the second round he stunned the crowd by performing a double backflip. This is a trick few skaters can manage. The fact that he can manage such tricks so smoothly earns him very high scores. All of his routines include flat spins of some sort. These are difficult tricks for most skaters, but Khris makes them look effortless.

Unfortunately, skating is a physically demanding sport, and it can take its toll on an athlete. Most aggressive competitors have suffered their share of injuries. Taïg Khris is no exception. In 2002, he was unable to compete in the X Games. He had performed several astounding tricks in the Gravity Games in July—including a double backflip, a Liu Kang 720, a double backflip 180, and a miraculous double flat spin—but he had hurt himself in the process. His injury was not yet healed, so he was forced to withdraw from the event, even though he had been one of the top two qualifiers. Fortunately, hard work and focused physical therapy paid off, and Khris was able to return to active competition the following year.

CHAPTER SIX
TODAY AND BEYOND

For some people, winning medals and prize money is enough. For others, it's all about naming a trick that people continue to use. Still others, though, want a different kind of fame. This kind of fame comes from being on television or in a video game. Over the last few years, more and more companies have been producing sports-based computer games, and often these involve real athletes. The companies pay the athletes for their likenesses and information and use that to create characters and moves so that the consumer can "play" the athletes. It's considered a

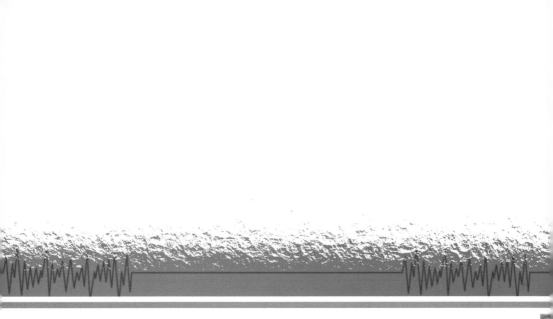

Taïg Khris has made it his mission to promote the sport of aggressive in-line skating to an international audience.

● ●

major step for an athlete to be invited to participate in a computer game, because only someone who is thought of as one of the stars of that sport would be considered.

Aggressive Behavior

In 2002, video game maker Acclaim released its newest game, *Aggressive Inline*, for the Playstation 2 game console. The game was all about in-line skating and focused on playing the various pros. Taïg Khris was featured promi-nently in the game. Acclaim approached him after it

Famous Tricks

Taïg Khris is best known for two things: the flat spin and the double backflip. He was single-handedly responsible for bringing the flat spin out of obscurity, when he perfected the 540 flat spin at the 1997 X Games. Other in-line skaters followed his lead, and soon the flat spin was a favorite trick for the top athletes. Khris was the first skater to land a perfect double backflip at the 2001 Summer X Games. Other skaters have since managed this trick, but Khris will always be remembered as the one who started it all.

developed its Dave Mirra stunt bicycle game. Acclaim offered Khris the chance to get involved in the development of *Aggressive Inline*. He helped the company refine the characters, the sets, and of course, the tricks. All of the tricks were done with motion capture, so the skaters actually performed them and then their motions were translated into the computer. That meant that every trick in the game was real and had been performed by the featured pro. Each character also had an ultimate trick. Khris's was his winning double backflip.

The game did extremely well and made even more people familiar with in-line skating and with Taïg Khris, in particular. Khris himself said that he actually learned new tricks from watching and playing the game, because seeing the movements on the screen inspired him to try new things.

Taïg Khris, Entrepreneur

Some athletes succeed because they focus all their time and energy on their sport. That gives them tremendous focus. This often means they don't have many other interests. When they become tired of the sport or get too old or injured to be a top competitor anymore, they may not have anything to fall back upon.

Those are not problems for Taïg Khris. For one thing, he has a variety of interests. In addition to skating and street magic, he also plays tennis (and was once a champion player), dances (salsa), and plays piano. Khris also has business interests.

Khris runs a skating school for Club Med. It's called the Taïg Khris Ramp School, and it's located at Club Med's Sandpiper resort, in West Palm Beach, Florida. The school has its own half-pipes and other ramps and more than enough space to accommodate a large group. Club Med members can sign their children up to participate. Khris runs the classes himself and teaches these young skaters about the sport. It's less about competition than about learning how to skate, how to manage a few basic tricks, and how to have fun in the process.

Khris also has his own skate shop. Located on the Allée Vivaldi in Paris, the shop is called Ilios. Khris runs the place himself, and in addition to the latest skates and skating gear, he offers skating classes and roller hikes in nearby Vincennes.

As if two businesses were not enough, Khris also owns his own ramp company. After all, he began building

his own ramps back when he was a kid wearing roller skates. Now he has a lot more experience. Who better to build a ramp than someone who spends all of his time riding on them? He even built himself a large ramp, so that he would have something to practice on. But it was too big to fit inside any place in Paris, and he didn't like the weather in either Paris (too rainy) or Germany (too cold). So he found a small village in Greece, Evian, and moved the ramp there. Now he lives in Evian part-time and skates there with the local children whenever he is around.

INJURIES

Every professional athlete has been hurt at some point in his career. For Taïg Khris, that time came in 2002. He was injured while competing at the Gravity Games and tore two ligaments, one in his shoulder and one in his knee. The wounds kept him off his skates for ten months, and he had to back out of the X Games that year because he was unable to skate. He spent all that time going to physical therapy, healing, resting, and working on other activities. These included his budding acting career and his new skate park. He admitted that it was difficult to recover from his injuries and even harder to take such a long break from skating and then try to get

Don't try this at home! Khris, without his protective gear, flies high above the heads of Alexander Wurz and Giancarlo Fisichella before the San Marino Formula One Grand Prix in Imola, San Marino, Italy, in 1999. Injuries in 2002 brought Khris down to earth, but not for long.

Career Highlights

It's difficult to pinpoint the high moments in Taïg Khris's career because it has been so consistently impressive. He has won a medal at the X Games every year from 1997 to 2001. His first year in competition, 1997, he was ASA Ranking Champion of the Year and Rookie of the Year. In 1999, he won first place in the ASA Awards. In 2000, Taïg was ASA World Champion. In 2001, he was the first in-line skater to win a Grand Slam— he won the X Games, the Gravity Games, the World Championship, the Bercy, the European X Games, and the World Team Challenge. That same year, he was ASA Skater of the Year and won for the Best Trick of the Year (the double backflip, which has

Khris celebrates after his final run in the In-line Vert competition during the August 2002 Gravity Games in Cleveland, Ohio.

become one of his two signature moves). Both 2002 and 2003 were more difficult, because he was recovering from injuries, but Khris has continued to place in events like the Euro X Games, the ASA, and the EXPN Invitational. And he has still won a medal in almost every event he has entered.

back into the competitive mindset. But he focused on the skating itself rather than the business or fame, and he worked his way back up to full strength and his former precision and grace.

In March 2002, Khris took part in a new event, the Taz Atti-Tour. This interactive tour featured popular Looney Tunes characters alongside top BMX bikers, skateboarders, and in-line skaters. The athletes all demonstrated their skills for the audience and also offered classes to local kids. The tour provided an open skate park for kids and pros alike, amateur competitions, video games, music, autograph signings, and other activities. It was sponsored by ASA Events, and Khris got the chance to perform with his own peers (like Shane Yost and Jaren Grob) but also with athletes from the other extreme sports (like bikers Jason Davies and Jimmy Walker and skateboarders John Comer and Richie Lopez).

Khris also has other interests outside of skating. His father was a theater actor, and Khris has gotten interested in the craft himself. He has begun taking acting classes and is supposed to appear in two films soon. Neither role involves skating, because he says he does not want to be typecast.

Words of Wisdom

Taïg Khris teaches skaters at various camps and has always been very encouraging to younger skaters and those interested in the sport. He encourages them to follow their hearts and take up the sport they enjoy most, because if they really like it they can't help but be good at it. Khris

Timeline

July 27, 1975 Taïg Khris is born in Algeria.

1981 Khris first tries on roller skates.

1990 Khris attends his first competition.

1996 Khris switches to in-line skates.

1997 Khris participates in his first in-line skating competition. Rollerblade signs him to its team.

In a short amount of time, Khris has achieved a lot for himself and the sport he loves.

Khris wins ASA Rookie of the Year and ASA Ranking Champion of the Year.

1998 Khris comes in second at the Gravity Games.

1999 He wins first place in the ASA Awards and first place in the Gravity Games.

2000 Khris becomes ASA World Champion.

2001 He wins the first in-line Grand Slam, becomes ASA Skater of the Year, and wins Best Trick of the Year (double backflip).

2002 Khris is injured at the Gravity Games and has to withdraw from the X Games.

2003 Khris returns to active competition.

says on the Club Med Web site, "When you love the sport you've chosen, you do it better than anyone else."

Khris also warns his students not to use a trick until they know they've mastered it: "I know I am ready to put a trick into my run when I have done it over and over again. If you want to win, you know you cannot put a trick in your run you are not confident with."

In the meantime, Taïg Khris has more than enough to keep him busy. He lives in Paris part of the time and Evian the rest, manages his skate shop when he is in Paris, goes to Club Med to practice skating and to teach his skate school, and keeps entering—and winning—competitions. He has been featured on various television stations, including ESPN, Fox, and the BBC, and he has a number of Web sites devoted to him and his tricks. In interviews, he has said that he wants to keep skating as long as he can. But he does have the other businesses, so even when he eventually retires from active competition he can stay involved in the skating world. It's something he enjoys a great deal, and he likes being able to give back to the sport by bringing in more people and helping them to appreciate and enjoy it. One of the ways he's doing that is by performing a demonstration at the 2004 Olympic Games opening ceremony in Athens, Greece. In-line skating is not yet part of the Olympic competition, but with people like Taïg Khris constantly amazing everyone with fantastic tricks, it may just be a matter of time before people see the sport as a medal event.

GLOSSARY

half-pipe A type of ramp used for jumps and
   airborne tricks.

in-line skates A type of skate in which the wheels are
   all in a single line beneath the center of the foot;
   also called Rollerblades.

quad skates Traditional roller skates, in which the
   wheels are set in two pairs beneath the foot.

roller skate A skate with wheels instead of blades (as
   in ice skates).

street A type of skating that uses a mostly flat course
   rather than ramps.

trick A specialized maneuver; a series of specific actions
   that combine into a single larger stunt.

vert Stands for vertical; it can also mean a ramp that
   has a vertical portion above the curve.

International In-line Skating Association (IISA)
National Office
201 North Front Street, Suite 306
Wilmington, NC 28401
(910) 762-7004
e-mail: director@iisa.org
Web site: http://www.iisa.org

International Roller Sports Federation
Rambla Catalunya, 121, 2-3
08008 Barcelona
Spain
e-mail: info@rollersports.org
Web site: http://www.rollersports.org

Skatelog.com
Web site: http://www.skatelog.com

National Museum of Roller Skating
4730 South Street
P.O. Box 6579
Lincoln, NE 68506
(402) 483-7551, ext. 16
Web site: http://www.rollerskatingmuseum.com

Web Sites

Due to the changing nature of Internet links, the Rosen Publishing Group, Inc., has developed an online list of Web sites related to the subject of this book. This site is updated regularly. Please use this link to access the list:

http://www.rosenlinks.com/exb/tkhr

FOR FURTHER READING

Brimner, Larry Dane. *Speed Skating*. New York: Children's Press, 1997.

Christopher, Matt. *Inline Skater*. New York: Little Brown & Company, 2001

Miller, Liz. *Get Rolling, the Beginner's Guide to In-line Skating*, Third Edition. Danville, CA: Get Rolling Books, 2003.

Nealy, William. *Inline! A Manual for Beginning to Intermediate Inline Skating*. Birmingham: Menasha Ridge, 1998.

Powell, Mark and John Svensson. *In-Line Skating*. Second Edition. Champaign, Ill.: Human Kinetics, 1998.

Publow, Barry. *Speed on Skates*. Champaign, Ill.: Human Kinetics, 1999.

Rappelfeld, Joel. *The Complete In-Line Skater: Basic and Advanced Techniques, Exercises, and Equipment Tips for Fitness and Recreation*. New York: St. Martin's, 1996.

BIBLIOGRAPHY

"Airtight Sports Interview." BBC. Retrieved August 12, 2003 (http://www.bbc.co.uk/scotland/sportscotland/airtight/in-line/interviews/taïg_khris.shtml).

Burns, Brian. "Khris Flips for Gold." Gannett News Service. Retrieved August 12, 2003 (http://www.delawareonline.com/newsjournal/sports/specials/xgames/news/0818khris.html).

Crecente, Brian D. "Game Teaches Old Skater New Tricks." Geek.com. Retrieved August 12, 2003 (http://www.geek.com/news/geeknews/2002may/bga20020521011794.htm).

Era, Colby. "1999 Pro Tour—Toronto Vert." Retrieved August 15, 2003 (http://www.asaskate.com/protour/protour99/toronto/toronto2.html).

"Gear Up! Guide to In-line Skating." Retrieved August 12, 2003 (http://www.iisa.org/gug).

"In-line Skating Guru Says Game Taught Him New Moves." Ananova. Retrieved August 9, 2003 (http://pda.ananova.net/entertainment/story/sm_589921.html?menu = entertainment.story).

"In-line Skating History." Xtreme Sports Center. Retrieved July 28, 2003 (http://www.tqnyc.org/NYC030417/html/in-linehistory.html).

"In-line Skating History—Roller Skating—Rollerblades." Kidzworld. Retrieved August 1, 2003 (http://www.kidzworld.com/site/p799.htm).

"Taïg Khris." Acclaim.com. Retrieved August 7, 2003 (http://www.akaacclaim.com/aggressiveinline/bios/khris.html).

"Taïg Khris." Club Med. Retrieved August 2, 2003
(http://www.clubmedpress.com/
article.php3?id_article = 102).

"Taïg Khris." EXPN.com. Retrieved August 12, 2003
(http://expn.go.com/athletes/bios/KHRIS_TAIG.html).

"Taïg Khris." Life Lounge. Retrieved August 9, 2003
(http://www.lifelounge.com/sports/in-line/
interviews/7.html).

"Taïg Khris." Talents. Retrieved August 5, 2003
(http://www.planet-talents.com/taïg-khris_gb.htm).

Yasutoko, Yuki. "Eito Yasutoko Completes the Ultimate
1080 Flat Spin!" Good Skates Chronicle. Retrieved
August 9, 2003 (http://www.hermosawave.net/b2/
1080 % 20Flatspin.html).

INDEX

A

Aggressive Inline, 47–48
Aggressive Skaters Association
(ASA), 27, 28, 33, 44, 52, 53

B

Bergeron, Jonathan, 44
Billiris, Manuel, 8
BMX, 16, 53

C

Chicago Skate Company, 13
Club Med, 27, 28, 49, 55

D

da Silva, Fabiola, 8

E

Edwards, Chris, 8, 37–38
Englehart, Marc, 37–38
ESPN, 34, 36, 55
extreme sports, 16, 17, 32

F

Fry, Tom, 8, 32

G

Gravity Games, 16, 27, 36, 38,
44, 45, 51, 52

H

Haribo, 27, 28

hockey, 13, 14–15
Hulgreen, René, 9, 44

I

in-line skates, 5, 9, 13, 14–15,
16, 27–29, 49
in-line skating, 5, 8, 9, 10,
13–16, 24, 25–27, 35, 36,
37, 40–43, 45, 47, 48
aggressive, 14, 17, 32–33
recreational, 14, 16

K

Khris, Taïg
competitions, 9, 24–25, 27,
32–33, 36, 43–44
early life, 6–7, 25, 27, 29–31
family, 6–7, 9
nickname, 29–31
sponsorships, 13, 24, 27, 28
stunts/tricks, 22–23, 25–27,
41, 43–45, 48

L

Longares, Marcos, 9

M

Merlin, John Joseph, 10–11
Mora, Cesar, 8, 32

N

Naegele Jr., Bob, 13

About the Author

Aaron Rosenberg is a freelance writer from New York.

Photo Credits

Front cover image, p. 37 © Icon Sports Media; cover (right), pp. 4, 24–25, 26, 30, 46–47 © Nicolas Sautiez/Corbis; back cover image © Nelson Sá; pp. 1, 10 (inset), 50 © Hulton/Archive/Getty Images; pp. 6–7 © Duomo/Corbis; pp. 10–11 © Eric Fowke/IndexStock; p. 12 © Roger Ressmeyer/Corbis; p. 15 © Edixon Gamez/AP/World Wide Photos; p. 17 © Michel Stringer/AP/World Wide Photos; pp. 18, 22, 32–33, 35, 54 © Tony Donaldson/Icon Sports Media; p. 20 © IndexStock; pp. 28, 40–41 © Roger L. Wollenberg/NewsCom; pp. 38, 42 © Larry Kasperek/Corbis; p. 52 © Al Fuchs/Corbis.

Designer: Nelson Sá; **Editor:** Mark Beyer; **Photo Researcher:** Peter Tomlinson